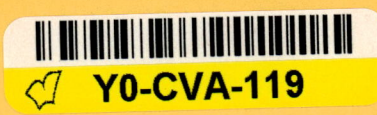

Designer: Julian Holland
Picture researchers: Caroline Adams, Ethel Hurwicz
Artist for Contents pages: Penny Thomson

Photo credits:
J. Allan Cash, 26-27; Douglas Dickins, 20-21;
David Holdsworth, 24-25; Featurepix, 4-5;
Spectrum Colour Library, 18-19, 28-29;
ZEFA, 6-17, 22-23, 30-31
Cover picture: ZEFA

© 1986 by Dillon Press, Inc. All rights reserved

Dillon Press, Inc., 242 Portland Avenue South
Minneapolis, Minnesota 55415

This edition published by Dillon Press by arrangement
with Macmillan Children's Books, London, England.
© Macmillan Publishers Limited, 1982

Library of Congress Cataloging-in-Publication Data

Snowdon, Lynda.
  Children around the world.

  (International picture library)
  Summary: Text and photographs depict children from
many countries at work and play. Includes a Dutch boy
in a festival and children at school in India.
  1. Children — Social conditions — Juvenile literature.
[1. Manners and customs]   I. Title.   II. Series.
HQ767.9.S64   1986   305.2'35   86-2021
ISBN 0-87518-338-7

International Picture Library

Children Around the World

Lynda Snowdon

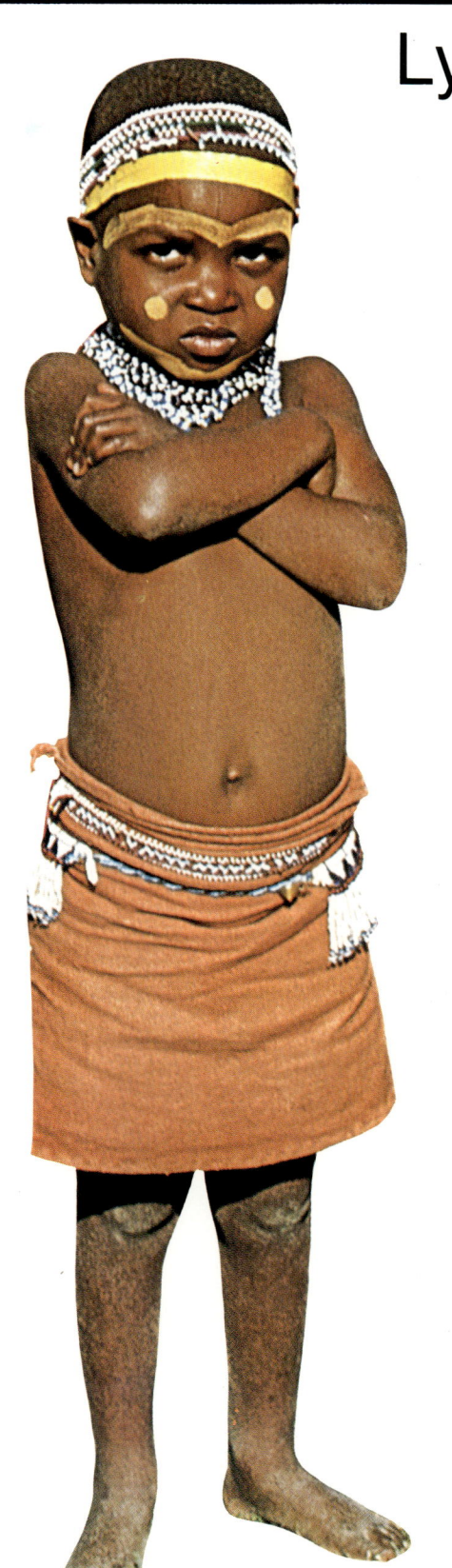

DILLON PRESS, INC.
Minneapolis, Minnesota 55415

Contents

10 Children in Bolivia

4 Austrian Girls

12 Brazilian Girls

6 A Dutch Boy in Fancy Clothes

14 Children in Morocco

8 Mexican Children at a Festival

16 A Boy in Tunisia

18 African Children after School

20 Boys in Nepal

22 Japanese Boys

24 A School in India

26 Indian Boys in the Punjab

28 Chinese Boys in a Park

30 Chinese Girls at a Festival

32 Countries Featured in this Book

Austrian Girls

These girls have been gathering flowers. Can you see the three different kinds of flowers? The girls have been picking

them in the fields near their homes. They live in a part of Austria where there are mountains. It is called the Tyrol and there are many forests there.

A Dutch Boy in Fancy Clothes
This boy lives in Holland. Once a year a festival is held in his town. The people dress up and parade through the streets.

The boy has put on a wig and painted his face with bright colors. Who do you think he looks like? Have you ever put on fancy clothes for a festival or party?

7

Mexican Children at a Festival
These children are at a folk festival near Mexico City. People have gathered to sing songs and dance the dances of

long ago. They wear traditional dress. Girls have always worn clothes like these to the festival. Their belts are woven and their blouses embroidered.

Children in Bolivia

These Indian children live in Bolivia.
Bolivia is a country in South America.
There are many mountains where the

children live. They and their families live on the mountainsides. Although it looks sunny, the air is cold. The children wear shawls and hats to keep warm.

Brazilian Girls
These girls live in Brazil. They usually wear skirts, dresses or trousers, but today they are at a festival. The clothes

they are wearing are worn on special occasions. The children paint their faces and wear pretty feathers. Their beads are made from dried seeds.

Children in Morocco
These children live high up in the mountains of Morocco. Their parents work in the mines or farm the fields.

The girls have their hair tied back. This keeps it out of the way when they are working. The scarves protect their heads from the hot sun.

A Boy in Tunisia

Have you ever had a ride on a camel?
This boy can have rides whenever he likes
because the camel belongs to his family.

The boy lives near the sea in a hot country called Tunisia. People go on vacation there. They like to ride camels. This camel gives rides along the beach.

African Children after School
These African children have just finished school for the day. Now they are going home, carrying their bags.

It is very hot. The road is dry and dusty and most of the children go barefoot. There are very few cars travelling along the roads here.

Boys in Nepal
In Nepal many boys go to school but only a few girls. This school is held in the open air. The boys keep books and

pencils in their school bags. In the north of their country there are many mountains. The highest mountain in the world is in Nepal. It is called Mount Everest.

Japanese Boys

When it is New Year in Japan there are many festivals. These boys are at one of the festivals. They follow each

22

other in a procession. Japanese boys wear clothes like these at the festivals. Japanese girls wear long dresses called kimonos. Everyone has a good time.

A School in India

More people live in India than in any other country except China. Many young Indian children go to school. They sit

on the floor and listen to the teacher.
Sometimes they sit at low tables and
play games like these children. Can you
see the number game in this picture?

25

Indian Boys in the Punjab
These boys are cutting up fresh grass and clover for buffalo to eat. It is hard work to keep turning the handle.

In this part of India many families keep a buffalo. They drink its milk and make any extra milk into a butter called ghee. They use ghee for cooking.

Chinese Boys in a Park
There are many beautiful parks in Chinese cities. These boys are sitting on a bench, playing a game.

People go to the parks to relax and to play sports. Most parks have an area where ball games like tennis and badminton can be played.

Chinese Girls at a Festival
These girls live in China. They have all dressed up for a special occasion. It is a flower festival.

In China festivals like this are held once a year. Baskets are decorated and beautiful flowers arranged in them. Many people come to see the displays.